IT WAS OVER WHEN...

TALES OF ROMANTIC DEAD ENDS

ROBERT K. ELDER

sourcebooks
casablanca

Published by Sourcebooks Casablanca, an imprint of Sourcebooks, Inc.
P.O. Box 4410, Naperville, Illinois 60567-4410
(630) 961-3900
Fax: (630) 961-2168
www.sourcebooks.com

Library of Congress Cataloging-in-Publication Data

Elder, Robert K.
  It was over when-- : tales of romantic dead ends / by Robert K. Elder.
     p. cm.
  1. Dating (Social customs)--Humor. 2. Mate selection--Humor. 3. Love--Humor. I. Title.
   PN6231.D3E44 2011
   818'.602--dc22

                                2010053372

             Printed and bound in the United States of America.
                    VP 10 9 8 7 6 5 4 3 2 1

To All the Girls I've Loved Before,
and to those who were kind enough to love me,
thank you, I'm sorry, and thank you.

Do you write in books you give as gifts? We do.

So here's space for your own story. You might even consider sending it to ItWasOverWhen.com, so we can immortalize your story on the Internet. Or in another one of these books.

....

....

....

....

....

....

....

....

....

....

....

....

....

....

CONTENTS

ACKNOWLEDGMENTS

First, thanks to our readers and contributors. Without your stories and enthusiasm, there simply would be no book, no website. Thanks for continuing to submit stories and helping spread the word.

My eternal gratitude goes out to Doug Peterson, the founding webmaster and tech guru behind ItWasOverWhen.com and ItWasLoveWhen.com. We spent a summer of extremely late, sleepless nights ironing out glitches and coping with overwhelming traffic, but he was always collected and cool. So thanks, Doug.

A special note of thanks goes out to my friends Jason Bitner, Andrew Huff, and Scott Smith, all of whom gave me invaluable early advice about the sites.

Thanks to filmmaker Kevin Smith (@thatkevinsmith) for writing early on about ItWasOverWhen.com on Twitter. You helped us go viral. And crashed the site.

Hats off to my friends for providing the first anonymous seed stories, which helped start the websites. Among them are: Marc Calvary, Adrienne Clem,

Lauren Graham, Esther Kang, Nicole Kristal, Autumn Whitefield-Madrano, Linda McCarty, Billie Oshana, Suzanna Naramore, Sam Parks, Becky Roberts, Bill Savage, Sasha Schwenk, Christine Whitmer Soileau, Shannon Terry, and Aaron Vetch.

I also had some help editing stories and running the websites from superstar editorial assistants Lisa Cisneros, Marcella De Laurentiis, Kasia Dworzecka, Kelin Hall, Samantha Leal, Theodore Nobel, Chelsea Trembly, and Emily Wray.

Thanks to Jon Resh for the amazing cover, which he furiously designed while expecting his first child. Special thanks to Anthony and Andrea Vizzari at 312photo booth.com for hosting our photobooth shoot!

Thanks to my editor at Sourcebooks, Shana Drehs, who believed in this book (and its forthcoming sister, *It Was Love When: Tales from the Beginning of Love*) and relentlessly pursued the projects. David Dunton, my tireless agent, is just too cool for words.

None of this, of course, would have been possible without the love, support, and good humor of my lovely bride, Betsy. The websites were built over my hobo summer, when I found myself unemployed and adrift at sea. She continues to be my compass home.

My wife hates this book.

She hated it when she was my girlfriend, hated it when she was my fiancée, and now hates it as my wife. (I've always thought that, perhaps, she feared being listed *in* it.) She says it's petty, mean, and a collection of stories about the straw that broke the camel's back.

She has a point, at least with that last part. This is a collection of epiphany moments, of the exact instant when you realize a romance is doomed—that you are, on some level, incompatible with your soon-to-be insignificant other.

But I don't believe these stories are mean or petty. They're very human stories.

These stories can be funny, sad, and sometimes both—but they're nearly always resonant, therapeutic, and universal. They make us laugh, cringe, sigh, and sometimes wonder what our exes say about *us*. Some are instructive, as much about ourselves and our expectations as they are a guide to navigating the land mine–riddled field of love. These stories feed our inner voyeur and show us how a romance can crash and burn over the tiniest details. The best stories tend to leave us wanting more. Some of them are raw and uneven, which makes them even more real and addictive. A few were edited for clarity, but mostly I've left them alone.

It Was Over When began as a game I started at parties, a chance to tell stories, laugh, and learn something about new friends. I gathered so many stories that it grew into a website and now, a book. In some ways, it serves as a chronicle of that ever-elusive thing we need as human beings to make us feel passion, comfort, and connection.

That's why *It Was Over When* has a sister volume, *It Was Love When*, which was inspired by my lovely wife. How we know we're in love is as important as recognizing when love (or the potential for love) ends.

I like to think that each of these stories has a happy ending—that each romantic misstep eventually leads to finding the right person, to a lasting love story.

I'm happy to say that's true for me. Some of the stories in here are mine. These car-wreck relationships (and a few that landed softly, amicably) ultimately led me to a woman who is both funnier and smarter than I am.

Yet, she hates this book.

I love her anyway.

WEIRD

THE SAMURAI

I walked into his room and found swords hanging on his walls—legitimate samurai swords. When I asked him about it, he had a distant look on his face, and said, "I am warrior." Not "I am *a* warrior"—just "I am warrior." Needless to say, I was frightened…and confused.

—Maddy

AFTERMATH

It lasted about two days after that. I gently ended it of course, after being a bit frightened for my life.

THE LEASE

After two years together, his lease was up for renewal. I suggested he and I move in together. His response: "You want to live with me and my roommates?"

—Mel

AFTERMATH

It lasted another six months before I realized he honestly and truly wasn't in this relationship for the long haul.

VICARIOUSLY

I was twenty years old and dating a high school teacher in his early thirties. I jokingly remarked one morning that I was not much older than some of his students, to which he replied, "I'm living vicariously through you because I can't lay a hand on any of them."

—Em

AFTERMATH

I bolted and never contacted him again.

DINOSAURS

HE THOUGHT THAT
DINOSAURS WERE A
CONSPIRACY THEORY.

—Noel

AFTERMATH

I PRETENDED I DIDN'T HEAR.

CAT WOMAN

As I waited patiently for her to get ready, her kitten started nuzzling me. I picked the cat up and realized the poor thing only had one eye. Then my date came in, grabbed the cat from me, and threw it violently onto the kitchen table, where it struggled to catch itself on the slippery surface before falling off the edge and landing on the hardwood floor.

—Leon

AFTERMATH

I rushed our date and broke up with her the next weekend.

ROCK OUT

My boyfriend told me he wrote a song for me and was going to play it at his next show. He came onstage screaming, wrapping the microphone cord around his neck like a noose, ripping his shirt off, and pouring fake blood on himself. He proceeded to properly dedicate it to his "hardcore girlfriend."

—Liz

AFTERMATH

We broke up…hardcore.

AL-ANON

She took me to Al-Anon, a meeting for the adult children of alcoholics, for a date.

—Aaron

AFTERMATH

That was the best part of the evening, even after she took off her clothes.

MANNEQUINS

He had two life-size mannequins in his living room, a man and a woman. They were dressed in the exact outfits his parents were married in (wedding dress and military uniform). I thought maybe his parents had passed and he was remembering or honoring them. No, they are still alive.

—Ricky

AFTERMATH

That was date number two; he didn't get to date number three.

THE CHECKLIST

She told me that I had passed her guy "date-ability" list, missing only one out of thirty-four requirements. I thought she was kidding until she showed me the actual checked-off list.

—LA boy

AFTERMATH

One week.

VAMPIRE

ONE NIGHT SHE
TURNED TO ME AND
SAID, "IT'S NOT
GOING TO WORK OUT,"
THEN BIT ME ON THE
ARM UNTIL I BLED.

—Bill

AFTERMATH

I NEVER SAW HER AGAIN. I
GUESS I WAS FORTUNATE TO BE
DATING A VAMPIRE WITH BAD AIM.

DOUBLE WHAMMY

My boyfriend told me he booked us a hotel room. When I arrived, I noticed ties on all corners of the bed, some lube, a blindfold, and a *cucumber*! I got a little freaked out after seeing all that. Then his cell phone rang. It was his wife.

—Rae

AFTERMATH

I have not returned any of his phone calls or text messages.

TWILIGHT SHAKESPEARE

Being well-read is a major turn-on for me. On the first date, I referenced Shakespeare's *The Taming of the Shrew* and *Much Ado About Nothing*, and she had never even heard of them. But she *had* read *Twilight*.

—Brian

AFTERMATH

There was not a second date.

CLOWNS

She had a framed picture of her and her mother both dressed in full clown outfits (orange hair, red nose, makeup, etc.) sitting on her kitchen counter. It freaked me out.

—Chris

AFTERMATH

I said good-bye.

ASPIRIN

She "attempted" suicide by eating two more than the recommended dosage of aspirin…

—Luis

AFTERMATH

Played along with it and talked her down until she agreed that suicide wasn't the answer. Was worried she might try it again with a harsher drug…like Flintstones chewable vitamins.

NEXT

I had just arrived to pick her up for our first date when her little boy ran over to me and said, "My mom says you are going to be my next dad." Yes, he said "next." We went out that night and never again.

—Dace

AFTERMATH

I ran into her a year or so later and found out she had gotten married but was getting a divorce, after only a year—her kid's new daddy number four.

PUPPY LOVE

ON OUR FIRST DATE,
IN THE MIDDLE OF
THE DANCE FLOOR, HE
LICKED MY FACE (FULL
TONGUE) FROM MY CHIN
TO MY EAR.

—Mandy

AFTERMATH

I NEVER SAW HIM AGAIN.

TOSSED HIS COOKIES

He was afraid the homemade cookies I brought him would make him fat. He said he would toss them as soon as I left, but not before adding, "No, I'll pee on them first."

—Amy

AFTERMATH

This story gets me sympathy.

SCRABBLE SMACKDOWN

He threw the Scrabble game
board across the room, tiles flying
everywhere, because I played a
word where he was planning to play
his *Q* word.

—Michelle

AFTERMATH

I threatened to break up, but he tried to show how much he loved me by reconstructing the board exactly as it was before his fit of rage. I married the arse, and later divorced him.

KNIGHT IN FUZZY CARPET

My parents just carpeted our downstairs and my boy-friend at the time asked me if we had any carpet left. So I said yes and gave it to him without thinking what he needed it for. The next day he showed up to school wearing the carpet in the form of armor. And wore it for the entire day.

—Shauna

AFTERMATH

We broke up soon after this happened.

PERCH

He kept climbing up on things. We'd go to a bar and he'd climb on the pool table or the bar or whatever else and perch on it. I think he thought it made him interesting, but it really just made him look like a tool.

—BlueCanary

AFTERMATH

He started wearing black eyeliner right around the same time I stopped returning his calls.

PLAYSTATION 3

We had been dating one and a half years when he told me one night that I was worth the equivalent of two PlayStation 3s to him. And really meant it.

—Chelsea

AFTERMATH

His friend told me later that he meant to say four. I ended it two months later; wish I would've done it sooner.

BIG BROTHER

I apologized after a fight. He forgave me, and gave me a comforting hug. A few minutes later, when I pointed out how sweet he was, he told me that he knew I couldn't help what I said because of the chip the government had implanted in my brain.

—Atta

AFTERMATH

I told him I was going to backpack Europe and left.

DADDY DON'T

She said, "You remind me of the fourth of my five fathers."

—QewlKat

AFTERMATH

Ran for the hills!

COOL CLUBS

He told me about a steroid patient he was treating in the ER for an infected abscess. He then told me that the patient was going to "hook him up and get him into some cool clubs" and that he took the patient's phone number. I laughed. It was not a joke.

—Heather

AFTERMATH

That was the last date. I dumped him via text about a week later.

WARLOCK

HE TOLD ME THAT HE WAS A WARLOCK AND HAD MAGICAL POWERS.

—Christy

AFTERMATH

I STAYED AS FAR AWAY FROM THIS MAN AS POSSIBLE.

SMOOTH 'N' SILKY

He said he shaves his legs because he likes the feel of it and women tell him it drives them wild.

—Lolita

AFTERMATH

It remains to be seen.

When I asked him who his best friend was, he said his ex-girlfriend. Who lived with him, who had left him for his other "best friend," who also lived with him.

—Anne

AFTERMATH

I gave it a sporting chance for about a month, but after that, it wasn't worth trying to play silver medal to his ex.

AFTERWARD

We were together for eight years. On our second wedding anniversary, he told me he was moving out and wanted a divorce. Then he asked if we could still date afterward.

—Amanda

AFTERMATH

The last time I voluntarily saw him was when we signed the divorce papers. Single life is hard for me, but it's better than being married to him.

CAESAR SALAD, MEDIUM WELL

SHE BOUGHT A GIFT FOR HERSELF AND PRETENDED IT WAS FROM ME. SHE ALSO HEATED HER SALADS IN THE MICROWAVE.

—Wolfman

AFTERMATH

WE DATED ONLY ABOUT A MONTH. THE GIFT WAS A BRACELET THAT SAID "LOVE."

SELF-DEFENSE

I kept a gun for self-defense because we lived in a shady neighborhood. One day he asked to borrow it. I asked why, and he said, "To kill my ex-wife."

—Spiralina

AFTERMATH

I changed my locks and eventually my phone number.

THE PEOPLE

After a few weeks, I finally got her to agree to a date. I made her dinner and we watched a movie. She ended up spending the night. She woke me up at 3 a.m. to ask me why I had let all the people in the room. There were no people in the room.

—Spally

AFTERMATH

She spent the next two days on my front porch. I ducked out the back of my house and went to stay with friends until I could get a friend of hers to come and convince her to leave.

WORLD'S GREATEST LOSER

MY BLIND DATE SHOWED UP AND
IMMEDIATELY GAVE ME A ROLLED-
UP PIECE OF FABRIC. I OPENED
IT UP, AND IT WAS A CALENDAR
WITH HIS PHOTO ON THE TOP AND
THE WORDS "WORLD'S GREATEST
LOVER." I GUESS I WAS SUPPOSED
TO BE EXCITED BY IT, BUT I
WAS EXTREMELY EMBARRASSED.

—KS

AFTERMATH

I did go on the date but I threw out the calendar as
soon as I got home. I never answered his calls.

FINAL, FINAL FANTASY

He started crying one night and told me he fell in love with a three-hundred-pound Canadian woman he met playing Final Fantasy online.

—Grateful He Sucked

AFTERMATH

I broke it off then. Three months later, he begged for me to take him back.

THE SHARTER

HE SHARTED
IN MY CAR.

—Melissa

AFTERMATH

IT SHOULD HAVE BEEN DUNZO
RIGHT THEN AND THERE BUT IT
LASTED A FEW MORE MONTHS.

BAD TIMING

I was in mourning over a kid who had died. The thought of dying so young got to me. I was crying on my boyfriend's couch, and he tried to console me. Then he put my hand on his crotch and tried to make me give him a hand-job while I was sobbing.

—Nicky

AFTERMATH

Thankfully, his grandmother came in so he threw my hand off. It lasted maybe three months afterward, and there is no justifying that duration.

TEA PARTY

I got up to go get a glass of water and came back into my bedroom to find my boyfriend on his knees proceeding to tea-bag my sleeping friend.

—Holly

AFTERMATH

I told him to zip up his pants and leave.

SERIAL KILLER

She told me she would swim to the bottom of the ocean for me. I replied, "But your head would explode." She said that was fine, if it were for me. Then I asked her if she would still love me if I was a serial killer. She said yes!

—Max Armbar

AFTERMATH

Needless to say, I did not kill multiple people to see if she was telling the truth. I just got the heck out of Dodge.

JUNK

I only knew the guy for a week when he asked if he could come to my place to see me. We were sitting on the couch watching TV (with family upstairs) when he all of a sudden pulled his junk out of his pants. In shock, I asked what the hell he was doing. His response: "Well, don't you want to suck on it?"

—Mandy

AFTERMATH

I kicked him out of my house immediately. He called every day not knowing he did anything wrong. I haven't spoken to him since.

POSTER CHILD

I SAW HIS BEDROOM FOR THE FIRST TIME—THE WALLS WERE COVERED IN MUSIC POSTERS, "COOL" CLIPPINGS FROM MAGAZINES, OLD CONCERT TICKETS, AND RANDOM SHOW FLYERS. DID I MENTION HE WAS TWENTY-EIGHT?

—Rae

AFTERMATH

We actually dated off and on for about a year before I finally broke it off for good. I always felt like I was thirteen in that bedroom—and not in a good way.

LAKE SUPERIOR

I met a girl at a bar where it was open bar. Dangerous stuff. We went back to her apartment. The next morning every square inch of the bed was soaked. Even the pillows were wet. It was either her, or me, or her fat angry cat. I suspect the cat. We didn't talk about the elephant in the room, or Lake Superior on her bed.

—Jack Diamond

AFTERMATH

There was no second "date."

I PREFER CREAMY

Not only did he have a man-purse (aka a "murse"), which I could have dealt with, but as we parted, he pulled a jar of chunky peanut butter out of his murse, gave it to me, and told me, "It reminded me of you."

—Missi

AFTERMATH

I tossed the peanut butter and never saw him or his murse again.

PUBES

He asked if I was seeing someone else. I said no and asked him why he would think that. He told me he was in my bathroom and found a male pubic hair in my toilet!

—Jennifer

AFTERMATH

I told him that if we had not had tickets to a show that night, I would *never* speak to him again, and after the show, I didn't. How he thought it was a male pubic hair, I will never know...

BITER

WHEN WE GOT BACK TO HIS PLACE, HE SAID, "I GOTTA SEE WHAT I'M DEALING WITH," AND BIT ME ON THE ASS.

—Mel

AFTERMATH

I NEVER SAW HIM AGAIN AFTER THAT NIGHT. I HEARD HE HAS A GIRLFRIEND NOW. HOPE SHE LIKES BITERS.

HAPPY DANCE

We were listening to Bob Dylan. Out of nowhere he jumped up from the sofa and danced around the room while pulling his hair, shaking his head from side to side, and shouting, "Yes!!" For three songs solid. When I asked what he was doing, he said: "It's how I express myself when I'm happy, and if you don't love my dancing then you don't love me…"

—Guys Shouldn't Bounce

AFTERMATH

I ended it soon after. If that was his "happy dance," I dread to think what being upset would do to him.

HANKY

During our date he proceeded to speak in different accents, tell me about his frequent visits to "massage parlors," and constantly pat his face with a hanky from his pocket.

—Ty

AFTERMATH

We lived an hour apart so I didn't feel obligated to see him again.

PHOTOGRAPHER

This girl took pictures of me—from I don't even know where—and spelled out her name and phone number with them and put them on the roof of my car.

—JJ

AFTERMATH

I did call her, only to tell her that I would call the cops if it ever happened again.

PENIS ENVY

He announced he was still traumatized from being circumcised and he wanted to "grow it back." He spent every day with his tiny unit wrapped in surgical tape and Popsicle sticks, with a lead weight dangling from it. Then he accused me of not wanting to have sex with him.

—Kat

AFTERMATH

I moved out. He was lousy in bed anyway, even when he wasn't wrapped like a mummy.

MAIL ORDER BABY

I was living in another state. She called me, wanting me to "collect a sample," freeze it, and send it to her so she could impregnate herself nine months before I got home. She thought it would be romantic to step off the plane and into the hospital for the birth of our "child."

—Katghoti

AFTERMATH

No sample, no baby, no more attachment.

I ALWAYS PUT IT THERE

On our first date we went back to his place to watch a movie. I went to use the restroom and there was a dildo in the sink. I shouted, "You left your dildo in the sink." He said, "Sorry," and said he was using it earlier.

—Tat

AFTERMATH

I left!

DOWN AND OUT

After going down on my girlfriend and giving her an amazing orgasm, she proudly said she wasn't going to return the favor because "I've gone down on lots of guys and never gotten anything in return. This is payback."

—Derrick

AFTERMATH

QUIT TRYING WITH HER.

JESUS OR MAGIC?

I can't decide…It was either when we were having sex and he pulled out, threw on his clothes, and said, "We can't do this; Jesus is watching," or when he told me we could never hang out on Sundays because that's when his Magic the Gathering card club met.

—Red Balloon

AFTERMATH

He broke up with me about a week after the sex incident, saying we were "going too fast" and that he needed to be more mature for his mother.

I ASKED HIM WHAT
HIS SEXUAL FANTASY
WAS, AND HE SAID,
"TWO REDHEADS."
I'M A BRUNETTE.

—Autumn

AFTERMATH

HE LEFT ME TWO MONTHS LATER.
FOR A BLONDE.

HUSH

While in bed, I complimented one of his (only success-ful) sexual moves. He told me I was "ruining his concen-tration." He *shushed* me during sex!

—Jen

AFTERMATH

It was over before he was finished!

ANATOMY LESSON

We were lying in bed after sex, and she asked if I knew when a female is ovulating. Obviously no, I'm a guy. She wiped her vagina, then rubbed her hand across my chest. She was explaining the thickness of the mucus when I dressed and walked out of the room.

—Jim

AFTERMATH

I didn't talk to her for a couple days after that. Finally I called and broke it off with her. Not my usual style but I didn't want to risk another anatomy lesson.

THREE-WAY TEASE

She was always teasing me with a three-way, with another girl. But when she came home with her new best girlfriend, they had no interest in me.

—Ricky

AFTERMATH

Divorced six months later.

WHAT COUPLES DO

Less than a year into our relationship, I asked her why she didn't seem to want to be around me in any way. No sex, no contact of any kind. She told me, "That's what couples do: they stop having sex."

—Aaron

AFTERMATH

She ended the conversation by summoning her dog to once again sleep in bed between us. I got jealous of that dog. She cried when I tried to break up. Later, she broke up with me when she found another boyfriend to share the rent.

BUZZ OFF

I realized, as he was taking his pants off and thrusting toward me, that the reason I wasn't attracted to him was because with his big round belly and hard dick, he looked like a bee coming at me with its stinger.

—Franny

AFTERMATH

It lasted less than two weeks after that. We never had sex again.

BOOKMARKED TAB

I asked to borrow his computer. His bookmarks tab was open and one of the pages he had bookmarked was "Chicks with Dicks."

—Lindsey

AFTERMATH

Our six-month "open" relationship ended about a month after this.

OFF THE MENU

ABOUT SIX MONTHS INTO THE RELATIONSHIP, SHE TOOK A PARTICULARLY *HOT HOT HOT* SEXUAL ACT OFF THE MENU. "THAT SHIP HAS SAILED," SHE SAID.

—Perry

AFTERMATH

SO DID I.

MOOD KILLER

We were about to have sex when he darted over to the computer to put on some "mood music" (his words, not mine) and got distracted by his gaming buddies on ICQ. I finally got his attention and we got down to business, but every time the ICQ alert would sound, it would completely throw him off rhythm. When we were done, he all but ran to the computer, presumably to tell all his friends what a girl was like.

—BlueCanary

AFTERMATH

Cheated on him a week later and ended it the next day. At least the break-up sex was good.

I asked him why he didn't pay anywhere near as much attention to my genitals as I did his. He said because it "grossed him out" to look at, touch, and especially put his face anywhere near vulvas/vaginas. It was made for the penis, and nothing else should go there.

—M

AFTERMATH

We communicated a couple times via instant message the week after, but never said another word to each other again.

MAN

He was way into the Society for Creative Anachronism and wanted me to join because I owned a horse and his "kingdom" needed a jouster. I dumped him when he mandated that we only speak in the King's English to each other.

—Anastasia

AFTERMATH

Last I heard, he thought he was a neo-romantic a la Bryan Ferry. At least he's in this century now.

WELCOME TO THE FAMILY

He brought his ex-wife to our dinner date. Not only was her name the same as mine, but he explained that they were looking to complete their family. He then proceeded to tell me the rules of the house and punishment for breaking those rules (something about flogging). Yeah, that wasn't happening.

—Jenn

AFTERMATH

They are still looking for their third!

THE GIGGLER

He giggled after sex. And not just a little—it was pretty hearty giggling. Like someone just told the funniest damn joke and it lasted for about five minutes. It was some kind of "tic" that he had. He couldn't control it and it happened to him every time.

—No Sense of Humor

AFTERMATH

I tried to give it a shot; he was a nice guy and I didn't want to be shallow. But I couldn't take it. A couple weeks and a few more "giggle" sessions later, I stopped responding. It was just too weird!

GIRLS

After a year of what I thought was a pretty strong relationship, she suddenly decided she wanted to see other people. "What other people?" I asked. "Girls," she replied.

—Jeff

AFTERMATH

It pretty much ended right then and there, although it took her two weeks to get all of her crap out of my apartment.

SNIFFER

I came home a couple of days early from a trip and caught him masturbating while sniffing my underwear.

—Christine

AFTERMATH

I stayed at a friend's house that night and started apartment-shopping first thing in the morning. I let him keep the thong as I won't be needing it again.

STILL NOT SURE

WE HAD SEX AND I
COULDN'T TELL IF HE
HAD AN ERECTION.

—Pilar

AFTERMATH

NEVER HEARD FROM HIM AGAIN
AFTER I INTIMATED THAT HE HAD
A SMALL, FLACCID PENIS.

RAPTURE

We were in the shower together before breakfast. I turned around to rinse my hair and saw his eyes rolled into the back of his head with a look of joy and rapture on his face. His mouth was slightly agape and his finger was in his own bottom. My God…the look on his face.

—Jana

AFTERMATH

It lasted long enough for me to rinse my hair and make an excuse to skip breakfast.

BIG BABY

I wouldn't do a certain position because I was pregnant. He threw a huge tantrum like he was five years old.

—Nika

AFTERMATH

Broke up with him the next day. Can't deal with a baby when I'm about to have a baby.

BIRTH CONTROL BRAT

We'd dated a few weeks when he told me that he refused to wear a condom, and that the ring (which I had) was the wrong kind of birth control because he'd be able to feel it during sex.

—Annie

AFTERMATH

He stopped returning my calls. We still bump into each other and it's awkward.

WATCH THE DRESS, BUDDY

HE TRIED TO GIVE ME
A GOLDEN SHOWER IN
A PARKING LOT AFTER
MY UNCLE'S WEDDING,
WHILE I WAS STILL
IN A PRETTY DRESS.

—Linda

AFTERMATH

I LEFT HIM IN MICHIGAN TO
FIND HIS OWN WAY HOME, BACK TO
INDIANA. ENDED THE NEXT DAY.

MOFO

He said he has never had better sex than the sex he has with my mother in his mind.

—D

AFTERMATH

We drifted apart, but I actually attended his wedding a few years later.

MR. CLEAN

I was dating an Austrian man. After sex, I asked him why he spent so much time in the bathroom before returning to bed, and he said, "I had to vaash my genitals."

—Lolita

AFTERMATH

It ended one month later, which was one month too long.

WITHER

Halfway through sex, my boyfriend looked at the clock and said, "Oh crap, it's 4:25—my crops are going to wither!" and proceeded to go to the computer to harvest his crop on Farmville, an online game.

—Sandra

AFTERMATH

I left and never went back.

BIOLOGY LESSON

He asked if the blowjob I gave him the night before could have gotten me pregnant.

—Ann

AFTERMATH

I spent a couple of weeks in denial before I finally broke it off, but I felt so much better once I did.

KEGEL HOMEWORK

We were having sex, and he asked me if I could "tighten my sh*t up." I hopped off. He kissed my shoulder and passed out drunk.

—He was a good kisser

AFTERMATH

Never talked to him again.

WHAM, BAM

Ten minutes into sex she says, "Why haven't you cum yet?" I said, "Because I don't want to yet." She shouted, "YOU MEAN YOU'RE DOING IT ON PURPOSE! I'm not the kind of woman who likes being here all night."

—Smooth

AFTERMATH

We broke up. It wasn't worth taking my clothes off for two minutes.

ONCE, OK...TWICE?

DURING SEX, SHE
CALLED ME BY
THE WRONG NAME.
WORSE, IT WAS HER
ROOMMATE'S NAME.
THEN SHE DID IT
AGAIN. ALSO, HER
ROOMMATE WAS GAY.

—John

AFTERMATH

THAT WAS ABOUT IT FOR ME.

SEX DRIVE

I was going down on this girl, working pretty hard, and all of a sudden she says, totally deadpan, "I would really be enjoying this if my medication didn't kill my sex drive."

—Tom

AFTERMATH

I finished the deed that night, but broke off contact shortly thereafter.

HAMPERED

He suggested we have sex and I agreed, if he had protection. He stood up, dug through his laundry hamper, and pulled out a condom that was already opened and unrolled.

—Allison

AFTERMATH

I never slept with him, though we continued seeing each other for a month because I felt bad.

IN AND OUT

I lost my "virginity" to a guy who performed the entire act to completion, not realizing he was never actually "in."

—Dawn

AFTERMATH

I broke up with him the next day, and he drove to my house and handed me a very angry letter that stated that girls who break up with a guy after what we did get a *very* bad reputation. He ended up with the bad reputation. Amateur!

TMI

After a mind-blowing round of oral sex, she said, "I can tell you eat a lot of fruit."

—Sweet tasting

AFTERMATH

She had been with too many men for my taste.

SECRETS

MAKE-A-WISH

He pretended to be the father of a terminally ill child to get a free vacation to Disney World out of the Make-A-Wish Foundation.

—Bobby

AFTERMATH

It lasted a week while I figured out the best way to break up with him without him wanting to ruin my life with harassment.

ROOMMATE KISS

It was over the minute his roommate kissed me. It just took me two years of bulls*** and misery to realize it.

—BlueCanary

AFTERMATH

Roommate and I have been together for three years now. (He thinks it's only been two.)

WORLD TRADE CENTER

He told me he was on the phone with someone in the World Trade Center during the 9/11 terrorist attacks and then saved people in a stranded subway train, and then had qualified for several Ironman triathlons, and was in a ten-car accident, and…

—Lolita

AFTERMATH

I tried to break up with Mr. Pathological Liar without saying why. We broke up and he continued to track me for a couple of years.

LESBIAN AVATAR

My husband was in an online game using a female avatar and fell in love with another player, also a female avatar. They had a wedding ceremony online in which my husband proudly proclaimed he'd never loved anyone the way he loves her.

—Barbara

AFTERMATH

Haha! Not only was my husband's avatar piloted by a man—so was the other "woman." We're divorced now and I hear my ex is pursuing a sex change.

IMAGINARY SISTERS

Some girls called asking for him,
claiming to be his sisters.
He didn't have sisters.

—Diana

AFTERMATH

I scratched all of his CDs and never spoke to him again.

THE BABY-SITTER

HE CHEATED ON ME WITH HIS OLD BABY-SITTER.

—Lisa

AFTERMATH

EWWW.

9 TO 5

We met at a party. He was well-dressed, smart. There was dating, good sex. I asked why he didn't work 9 to 5. He told me of his scheme that involved retail white-collar theft and eBay. Then he finally told me about prison. He got charged in new felonies and tried to get me to testify in his case. He had his lawyer harass me to perjure myself. Now he writes me flowery jail letters. I read them and laugh.

—PL

AFTERMATH

Lasted zero days after he was arrested. He is still in jail. He tried to get his cousin to sell me his truck for bail money, but then wouldn't sign over the title.

EXOTIC MASSAGE

My friends were going through the (gay) exotic massages and other sexual offers on Craigslist and laughing at how funny some of them sounded. They got to one that had a familiar number. It was my boyfriend's number.

—Jane Doe

AFTERMATH

Had a guy friend set up a time and place to meet him. I was there too and broke up with him.

RANDOM GIRL

He spent the night out at a "friend's house" after ignoring my phone calls all day. He told me that he "didn't think I'd care" that my live-in boyfriend "got drunk and passed out" at some random girl's place.

—E

AFTERMATH

We broke up a month later, got back together, then broke up six months later when he decided he'd rather sleep with his graduate assistant than me.

EX WANK

I caught him masturbating to pictures of his ex-wife. They had been divorced for over six years and she's remarried.

—LO

AFTERMATH

HE WOULDN'T GET RID OF THEM SO I LEFT.

DIVORCE PAPERS

HIS WIFE CALLED ME TO FIND OUT WHERE SHE COULD SEND THE DIVORCE PAPERS.

—Ali

AFTERMATH

SHE AND I ARE FRIENDS. WHO KNOWS WHERE HE IS NOW?

HOOTERS

I came home during my last summer of law school and my boyfriend of five years told me he was sleeping with a Hooters girl.

—LL

AFTERMATH

The next day he asked me for legal advice. I guess that's not on the menu at Hooters. We haven't spoken since.

GOOD DIET

I figured out my girlfriend's unexplainable weight loss was due to her being a closet drug addict!

—Chuckie

AFTERMATH

Lasted for a couple of courtesy months.

CRAIGSLIST

I read an email of his that simply stated, "Yo bro, let me know next time you need your hot c**k drained." I have nothing against homosexuality, unless the man I'm dating is trying to hide it from me. And I'm a lady.

—NatahleyBee

AFTERMATH

He attempted to come up with an alibi. We are now broken up and I'm convinced he's getting anonymous BJs from Craigslist.

TATTOO

My boyfriend of three years told me that he had his new girlfriend's name tattooed on him. He told me this after we had sex.

—Brittany

AFTERMATH

It didn't last.

OUR TWINS

At a cookout, he shared with his boss that I was pregnant with twins and used that opportunity to ask for an increase in pay. I was not pregnant, did not look pregnant, and we had only been dating for a month at that time.

—Ma Shell

AFTERMATH

It ended that night. I saw his boss about a year later and he asked about our kids, as he got regular updates from my ex on how they were doing. I told the truth to the boss and the ex lost his job.

COUNTY FAIR CHEATER

We had been dating for five years and I was seven months pregnant when we went separately to the county fair. He had no idea I was there and saw him kiss another girl. He came home and asked why I was pissed. When I told him, he said, "Can't I have you both?"

—Shay

AFTERMATH

We ended our relationship. I'm marrying an amazing guy.

ROAD TRIP

My husband, my best friend, and I went to the beach one weekend, but along the way during the three-hour trip, we pulled into the parking lot of a nondescript brick building. Curious, I asked, "What's going on? Something wrong with the car?" I was told we had to stop to get an abortion for my best friend, and it was my husband's kid. The parking lot was for the clinic.

—*sigh*

AFTERMATH

We signed divorce papers a month later. They are now engaged and living together, and I'm happier than I've ever been in my life.

MIA

I found out he had gone MIA because he had been in jail. I stupidly took him back only to have him go MIA...again.

—Kate

AFTERMATH

I quit trying to pursue the "relationship," or lack thereof. I also found out that the entire time we had been dating, he was engaged.

GET OUT OF MY HOUSE

Three days after moving into a house we bought together (with my money), I found his online dating profile on the computer. He had been with someone just *two days* before we moved in together. He said we weren't in a committed relationship until we physically moved in together.

—Kellee

AFTERMATH

It took seven months, a call to the police, and the threat of a restraining order to get his name off the title of *my* house.

LIAR, LIAR

I found out that she gave me herpes knowingly and proceeded to lie about it for six months. She even let me go through the motions of letting me call people I was with before to tell them they may be at risk.

—Bob

AFTERMATH

I, like a fool, tried to forgive her. It was impossible. Also, she lied about sleeping with my best friend, and gave him herpes too.

DUI

He hid his DUI from me for months. Later, he almost threw me out of his house after I asked what I was to him after we'd been "dating" for four months.

—BaltOhNo

AFTERMATH

I slept with him off and on, and after two years of wanting him to fall in love with me, finally realized I needed to let go. It's amazing how great sex can cloud judgment.

THE KITCHEN

MY SON WALKED INTO THE KITCHEN AND MY FIANCÉ WAS HAVING ORAL SEX WITH A FRIEND OF MINE.

—Marcie

AFTERMATH

IT LASTED LONG ENOUGH FOR ME TO ALLOW HIM TO PACK HIS STUFF.

BLOATED

She could no longer hide the growing fullness of her belly. I had had a vasectomy three years earlier.

—James

AFTERMATH

Her lies revealed and my suspicions confirmed, she moved in with her baby-daddy.

HORSE WHISPERER

During our three-week relationship, his story went from "I raise show horses" to "my family raises show horses and I help" to "I live with my family and a bunch of old gimpy horses because I'm afraid to live by myself." He was twenty-eight.

—Boy's Mamma?

AFTERMATH

After I broke up with him and told him never to contact me again, he emailed, called, and came to my house seventy times in two months. I filed a restraining order.

TRAVELER

While she encouraged me to spend more time traveling, she was carrying on an affair with her boss. When I found out, she blamed me for not being around enough. She never even said she was sorry.

—Phil

AFTERMATH

Still married. When my daughter goes to college, I go out the door.

WITHDRAWAL

My quarterly savings account statement arrived, $800 light. I'd put his name on it for a just-in-case emergency (like my death). When asked about the withdrawal, his response was, "I was going to put it back before you found out."

—Trusted Gut

AFTERMATH

Three months later, I threw him out.

INSTANT CHEATER

I went to pick her up to go see a movie and went on her computer to check times. She left an AIM conversation open with her ex-boyfriend ending with them exchanging "I love yous." I closed the window before she saw what I was looking at.

—Jason

AFTERMATH

I confronted her about it a week later. I wanted to dump her and she deflected the blame on me.

FAMILY MAN

I was dating a guy long distance. After a few visits he told me he had something important to tell me. It turns out that he had molested two of his own children. His therapist told him that she wouldn't let him out of the state again unless he told me everything.

—Jen

AFTERMATH

He got mad that I didn't want to start a family with him (after three dates). We haven't spoken since.

PROFESSIONALS

NOT ONLY DID HE CHEAT, BUT WITH "PROFESSIONAL" WOMEN...

—Lisa

AFTERMATH

I AM HAPPILY DISEASE-FREE AND IN SOMEONE ELSE'S MONOGAMOUS BED.

WHAT IT LOOKS LIKE

I was in a two-year relationship and I was Christmas shopping with her eleven-year-old daughter. We came home early and caught her mother (my girlfriend) fellating a mutual friend. She took him out of her mouth and while still holding it said, "This isn't what it looks like." I told her I was taking her daughter to her mother's house and left.

—JP

AFTERMATH

Never spoke again. Her mother was horrified, as I had done CPR on her dad and saved his life a few weeks earlier. The child was mortified and still calls me five years later.

HINT GIFT

I GOT A "COOKING FOR ONE" BOOK FROM MY WIFE FOR CHRISTMAS.

—jake

AFTERMATH

I didn't get it until I found out she was dating someone else. Try not to talk to or see the tramp.

FIVE YEARS TO MAKE A MAN

Year one: We diet and go to the gym together.

Year two: He gets plastic surgery from all the weight he lost from year one.

Year three: He is happier and I push him for a new job, while I start house-hunting.

Year four: I buy him a laptop for Christmas and put the down payment on his new car.

Year five: My skinny, good-looking boyfriend uses his laptop to find a new girlfriend who he impresses with his new car and three-flat financial investment.

—Monika

AFTERMATH

I am living with a new boyfriend who I don't have to buy a thing for and I am the happiest I have been in five years. Lesson learned.

BLUSHING BRIDE

His new-to-me fiancée answered the door when I went to visit him, holding their six-month-old baby!

—Shay

AFTERMATH

I congratulated the blushing bride on her awesome pick of a husband-to-be.

IDENTITY THEFT

I'd been dating "David" for about six months and we were about to embark on a three-week vacation. A couple days prior to departure, his brother—*David*—calls me. Turns out, while he was overseas on a work assignment, his brother (the "David" I was dating) was "house-sitting." Basically, everything I knew was really part of the overseas brother's life and identity.

—Sharon

AFTERMATH

The real David had the fake David committed to the local mental hospital upon returning home.

BAILOUT

I hadn't heard from him in a couple of days so I checked his Facebook page. There I saw that his sister had posted a request to borrow $2,500 for three weeks to get him out of jail. Nobody in their family could help him.

—Susie

AFTERMATH

If they can't help him, I am not going to.

PERSONAL AD

I placed a fake ad on the personals page of a local paper pretending to be exactly the kind of guy I thought she'd like. The ad only got one response, and it was from my wife.

—Dave

AFTERMATH

I got custody of the kids and am happily remarried.

SHOPPING TRIP

I WENT GROCERY
SHOPPING AND RAN INTO
MY BOYFRIEND, HIS
WIFE, AND HIS CHILD.

—Letty

AFTERMATH

FOR THE CHILD'S SAKE I DIDN'T
MAKE A SCENE; I WALKED AWAY.
AN HOUR LATER HE CALLED ME AND
TOLD ME THEY'RE SEPARATING. I
HUNG UP ON HIM AND NEVER HEARD
FROM HIM AGAIN.

My best friend and I were talking about how excited we were that we were both pregnant, and she asked my advice on how she was going to tell the father of her baby—my husband.

—Maxxx

AFTERMATH

She didn't have her baby, and I got divorced.

QUIRKS

WHO'S YOUR DADDY?

She wanted me to dress up in her father's uniform and punish her for getting a "C" on her report card.

—Mr. E

AFTERMATH

I left and haven't talked to her since.

THERAPIST

She said, "I was talking to my therapist about you and she said…"

—AKK

AFTERMATH

It was over in two weeks.

OH LORD

HE CRIED DURING THE LAST *LORD OF THE RINGS* MOVIE.

—Kelly

AFTERMATH

HE CRIED WHEN I BROKE UP WITH HIM TOO.

SHOELACES

I was at the store one day and happened to remember that my skateboarding boyfriend said he needed a new pair of shoelaces. So in an attempt to be a thoughtful girlfriend, I bought him a pair...but it was apparently the wrong kind. When I brought them over the next day, his only response was, "If you can't pay attention to the kind of shoelaces I wear, how can I expect you to understand my needs?"

—L.

AFTERMATH

We were together off and on for about two years, but it was high school so that's pretty much an eternity.

TOO THRIFTY

An unfortunate event led me to meet a hippie chick as a blind date. I was halfheartedly listening to her spout off the many ways she was thrifty, an avid recycler, and a freegan who rummaged through back alleys for clothing and used the Mooncup Menstrual Cup (blech!). The world stood still for me when she said she did not use toilet paper. Instead, she used rags and washed them for reuse.

—Joshua

AFTERMATH

She sent emails, but I blew her off.

HIGH FIDELITY

While saying our vows, my soon-to-be-husband broke down in laughter. He couldn't, no matter how hard he tried, say the word "fidelity."

—Jane Doe

AFTERMATH

Five years later we divorced.

FISH SANDWICH

We went through the drive-thru window at a fast-food place and he ordered a fish sandwich and pronounced it "fill-ett o' fish." He wasn't joking and I knew he was just too stupid to continue the relationship.

—Alexa

AFTERMATH

I broke up with him a couple weeks later and it only lasted that long because the sex was good.

HE CRIED BECAUSE
HIS FAVORITE
BAND, SYSTEM OF A
DOWN, BROKE UP. HE
GOT ANGRY AT ME
BECAUSE I WASN'T
BEING EMOTIONALLY
SUPPORTIVE.

—Cynthia

AFTERMATH

WE BROKE UP A WEEK LATER, AND
HE STILL HOLDS A GRUDGE...FOUR
YEARS LATER.

HULKAMANIA

I came home and saw my husband working on some type of project. He was making a WWE wrestler belt out of an old pizza box, gold paint, and a Sharpie.

—Amber

AFTERMATH

He spent three days working on it. My dog got ahold of it, chewed it up, and he made another one. I divorced him shortly after, but I kept my dog.

DANCING QUEEN

I went to hang out at her house for the first time and was forced to sit and listen to ABBA's "Dancing Queen" on repeat for nearly an hour straight.

—Andrew

AFTERMATH

Needless to say, it ended the second I left her house.

HOT HALLOWEEN

Going to a costume party for Halloween, my boyfriend was incredibly more excited about he and his friend going as lesbians than me going as a Playboy Bunny.

—lemonlime

AFTERMATH

HE MIGHT NOT HAVE APPRECIATED MY COSTUME. BUT HIS FRIEND DID. A LOT...

LEGO LAND

I went over to his house for a chance to spend some romantic time alone. We ended up looking in his basement for his long-lost LEGO set, and I watched in amazement as he spent over an hour building himself LEGO architecture on the floor, smiling like an eight-year-old.

—Clo

AFTERMATH

I left his house early that night, and about a week later, I ended it and never looked back.

FIRST DIP, THIRD NIP

We went out on the lake and, after his first dip in the water, I noticed the mole on his chest had reacted to the cold. Triple nipple is a deal breaker.

—Jillian

AFTERMATH

The moment we hit land, I was out.

CAVITY CREEP

Our second date was dinner and live music at a popular sports pub. I'm kind of silly, and when I made him laugh with a crazy story, I noticed his black teeth!

—Joy

AFTERMATH

Deal broken.

PILL POPPER

He picked up and swallowed the pill he dropped from the pub floor as he was so desperate to have it, even though everyone else on the night out was only drinking.

—Helen

AFTERMATH

A couple weeks later he said, "Let's go on holiday." I said, "Let's break up."

LITTLE MISS SARCASM

I realized that she had only one setting: sarcastic. No seriousness, no deeper emotions, no ability to hold a decent conversation. Every response from her was some sort of joke, but it got to be too much.

—Scott

AFTERMATH

I put up with it for about a month. I love a little sarcasm, but there is a point where it goes from a funny little quirk to downright annoying.

IN DINOSAUR

AFTER ONLY TWO DAYS OF CHATTING ON FACEBOOK, HE TOLD ME, "RAWR! IT MEANS 'I LOVE YOU' IN DINOSAUR," AND HE WAS SERIOUS.

—KutcherGirl

AFTERMATH

NONE.

SHAPE

I woke up, looked at my partner sitting on the edge of the bed, and realized that I absolutely detested the shape of his head.

—Narie

AFTERMATH

It only lasted three months after that.

MUFFIN TOP

He explained that his friends at work liked to grab his "muffin top" that hangs over his jeans to tease him.

—Amy

AFTERMATH

I allowed him to take me on a few more dates because he had good taste in restaurants.

ONE LOVE

SHE SAID SHE HATED
REGGAE. SHE HATED
IT SO MUCH SHE
WOULDN'T TALK TO ME
IF I LISTENED TO IT
NEAR HER.

—J

AFTERMATH

I BROKE IT OFF BLARING "ONE
LOVE" BY BOB MARLEY.

BABY FOOD

One night on the phone she started telling me about all her little "quirks." It was so boring I stopped listening. I tuned back in to her monologue just in time to hear her say that she likes to eat baby food. As in little jars. As in Gerber…

—Spike

AFTERMATH

She eventually stopped calling me.

PIXEL GIRLFRIEND

Over our year-long relationship, we played video games together all the time, which was fine. The problem came when he canceled our actual in-person dates so we could play online from our respective homes. He liked my video-game character more than me.

—Nicole

AFTERMATH

A month later, he told me he could "never really love me."

CHEMISTRY

TEARS OF A CLOWN

My boyfriend said, "I think clown makeup is really sexy." Shortly thereafter, he whispered in my ear, "Seriously, babe, it's a major turn-on." He wasn't joking.

—Chelsea

AFTERMATH

I broke up with him that night. For the four months that we dated, I always thought he said and did really weird things to be goofy. He was definitely serious about all of it.

READER

We worked together at a bar and you know how that goes: sweaty work tensions can be relieved with sweaty play. One night after closing the place, we end up back at her studio apartment and go directly bed-wards, where things were marvelous. Afterward, as she slept, I had to use the bathroom and I noticed something very strange about her apartment. She didn't own a single book. Not one. Not even a thriller or a bodice-ripper or a *Reader's Digest Condensed Classic*.

—Will

AFTERMATH

That was that.

BIGFOOT

He got skunked in Beer Pong, a drinking game. The house rules dictated he had to run a naked lap through the woods. Seeing his naked body in the moonlight, I noticed that he looked a lot like photos of Bigfoot sightings.

—Summer

AFTERMATH

Long enough for me to find out that it's true that a man loses one inch of "manhood" for every ten pounds of extra weight.

CHAPEL OF DISCONTENT

WHEN WE ARRIVED AT THE WEDDING CHAPEL, NEITHER OF US MADE A MOVE TO TAKE OFF OUR SEAT BELTS.

—LB

AFTERMATH

WE CALLED IT OFF A WEEK LATER.

MY JEANS

He found my jeans on the floor and pulled them on, thinking they were his. They fit. And they looked kinda good. And he danced around in them for a second, reveling in the fit.

—K

AFTERMATH

We broke up for other, less ambiguously gay reasons not long after, but this is the horrifying moment I remember, over and over again…

THERE SHE IS!

On our third date, I met a guy at his house. He was showing me pictures in a photo album. When he came to a picture of himself, he said, "There she is, in all her finest!"

—Brian

AFTERMATH

We did not have a fourth date.

SWERVE

She spent our date telling me how she'd had an affair with our waitress, which was fine. That happens when you date a stripper—it's half the reason you date a stripper. But, when she took me home, she drove demon-fast, erratically, and sang over an ear-splitting stereo. She then flashed her breasts to the cars next to us while swerving into their lane.

—Rob

AFTERMATH

I never called her again, though she did show up at my house on her break, wearing a waist-length blonde wig. I turned her down gently, not telling her that she was two degrees too crazy for me.

INEXPERIENCED

It somehow came up in discussion that apparently I've kissed more girls than he has. And I've never even been into girls. I think he needs more dating experience before getting serious with me.

—Jen

AFTERMATH

I'm procrastinating about ending things. Maybe a break, or a breakup. I swear I've tried, but he's so cute…

NUMB

We were in bed spooning one
night, and my arm fell asleep
underneath her. As I went to slide
my arm out, she turned around
and said, "What's wrong with you?
Don't you love me?" She rolled
over and bawled for the next hour,
inconsolable.

—Michael

AFTERMATH

Two months later, we were through. After my arm fell
asleep, there was a constant boo-hoo over everything.
I couldn't take it.

HOOPS

We cuddled on the bed and watched TV when I noticed her large hoop earrings. I told her how nice they looked and she immediately responded, "I will make you jump through hoops for me," in her thick Russian accent. Those words, along with the accent, turned me off instantly. Her gorgeous looks couldn't save her.

—George

AFTERMATH

Two days after the comment she became the first and only girl I broke up with via text message.

PICTURE PERFECT

After a very dull first date, we went to his house where he pulled out photo albums and started showing me pictures of a camping trip with his ex-girlfriend. Even stranger: I was a total doppelganger for her.

—Elizabeth

AFTERMATH

I texted to cancel our next date. He called nine times, leaving four sad messages, the last of which was many minutes long, full of tears and "*Whyyyyy, Elizabeth, whyyy!*" I played it on speakerphone for my friends.

BEND AND SNAP

He constantly wanted to listen to "Legally Blonde: The Musical" and then did the "bend and snap" in front of one of my gay friends at a wedding. All I ever heard from my friends after that was how obviously gay he was.

—Ade

AFTERMATH

It lasted for another nine months. Ultimately ended because he cheated on me—twice. At least it was with a girl.

POCKET BIBLE

On our second date, he pulled out his pocket Bible and asked me what my favorite verse was. When I couldn't think of one, he read me his favorite one and preached to me about God's love for the rest of the night.

—Vivian

AFTERMATH

I went out with him one more time so he wouldn't think that his God talk scared me away. But it totally did!

EAU D' HOSPITAL

We had some drinks and went back to her apartment. I was blown away by her comfort in disrobing and how amazing her rack was. We had great sex...and then I noticed it. She had the peculiar smell of a hospital when she perspired.

—Diggity Dave

AFTERMATH

We met at the movies a week later. I *really* hoped it was something in her apartment, but as she hugged me at the theater, the hospital smell wafted up my nostrils for the last time!

GOALS

I asked him what he wanted to be doing in five years. He said, "Still driving a truck and finally be making real money at $15 per hour." He had already been working there for five years and had started the job at $13 per hour.

—Ma Shell

AFTERMATH

We lasted two weeks after that. And the clincher? When I had to give him a pen so he could sign my birthday card.

HE TOLD ME I
"TASTED LIKE
ASPIRIN" WHEN
WE KISSED.

—Cassie

AFTERMATH

I SHOULD HAVE KNOWN HE WAS
A JERK WHEN HE BROKE UP WITH
HIS GIRLFRIEND FOR ME.

GROUND FLOOR

He informed me that he would "be a millionaire someday" and I should "get in on the ground floor." I laughed. He wasn't joking.

—Jen

AFTERMATH

We never went out again, and he was subsequently convicted of felony theft and related charges.

TEAR-STAINED UNDIES

I only dated him because he was a cop and I thought he was hardcore. I told him it was over after three dates and he bawled like a baby in front of his mates in the bar, then stripped to his undies because he thought I was breaking up with him because he wasn't "wild" enough.

—MG

AFTERMATH

He stripped again in my apartment, in front of my flat-mates. Please God, that's enough.

LAST KISS

The first time we kissed, she bit my lip. I'm not opposed to nibbling, but she busted it open.

—Tony

AFTERMATH

Fifteen minutes.

WRAP PARTY

I went to a wrap party for a TV show he was working on and everyone I met kept commenting, half jokingly, to me about how I seemed too cool and nice to be engaged to such an a**hole (their word, not mine). After about conversation number five, a light went off in my head.

—Anastasia

AFTERMATH

I dumped him about a week later.

CAT MAN

IT WAS OVER WHEN
HE ASKED HIS CATS
WHAT I WANTED TO
DO THAT DAY. IN A
DOGGY VOICE.

—Mizz Gooch

AFTERMATH

I F***ING HATE CATS. ONLY
LATER DID I FIND OUT THAT HE
NAMED ONE OF HIS CATS AFTER
HIS FAVORITE PORN STAR.

COULD IT BE...HMMM...SATAN?

For months it was a roller coaster of ups and downs, breaking up and getting back together. I should have known it was *permanently* over when he said he didn't believe in evolution (I'm a scientist) and that gays were caused by Satan.

—KT

AFTERMATH

I think we stayed together for a few more months.

WILD KINGDOM

Before our first date, I entered her studio apartment to find a jumbled mess of cups, plates, clothing, and stuffed animals. She also had seven pets. She talked to them in a cooing baby voice the entire time she got ready.

—William

AFTERMATH

For some reason (I'm guessing it had to do with my libido) I chose to stay with her for over a year of bizarre behavior that included throwing pasta at my head because there was an ant on the plate. And then crying and banging her head on the wall when I got angry about it.

CULTURE SHOCK

He started making plans for a joint vacation (after only four days of knowing each other) to New York's Chinatown because he wanted "to learn more about my culture." I'm Korean.

—Anem0ne

AFTERMATH

HE WAS A VERY CLINGY, STICKY RICE QUEEN, SO IT WASN'T TOO DIFFICULT QUITTING HIM.

FAVORITE ENDEAVOR

We argued for an hour about anal sex. Apparently, this was a favorite endeavor of his and his ex-girlfriend and he was insistent that I engage in this act as well.

—Lee-Lee

AFTERMATH

Two weeks later I went by his house at 3:30 a.m. and found his ex-girlfriend's car parked outside.

CLASHES

EARTH FIRST

We were talking after sex one night, and she mentioned that the environmental movement was a secret government plot to keep us scared and obedient. I'm am energy efficiency consultant and activist who takes my impact on the Earth very seriously. I asked her if she knew what her statement meant for me. She responded, "Well, you can't blame me if you're wasting your life."

—Randy

AFTERMATH

After coming to terms with the fact that she was dead serious, I asked her to leave. It was midnight and she lived fifty miles away, but I couldn't stand the thought of wasting another minute of my life with her.

DIMINISHING RETURNS

We were fighting one day and he drew me a graph on his whiteboard of hours spent together vs. utility derived from the relationship. He argued that us going on nice dates is just as good as him sitting on my couch playing video games for eight hours. Not only did he graph our *relationship*, he completely missed the concept of diminishing marginal utility. Good job, econ major.

—Peaches

AFTERMATH

We broke up the next morning, and were on and off for a few more months. Maybe his social sciences improved with the next girl.

FUTURE GREETER

She told me her goal in life was to retire from Wal-Mart. I responded along the lines of "You're joking, right?" She hung up on me, and then wouldn't answer the phone. When I stopped by her house, her mother answered the door saying, "She don't wanna talk to you, you've upset her..."

—Doug

AFTERMATH

I never saw her face-to-face again, recovered the few items I left at her place, and only look back to laugh at how happy I am that I've moved on.

STARTING OVER

My boyfriend of nine years told me he would never leave me because, "As hard as this relationship is, it would be harder to start over with someone else."

—Tofu

AFTERMATH

I stayed for another year before realizing what an ass he was.

IT WAS WRONG

I walked out of my house to find a letter on my car wherein he wrote that he could not continue the relationship any longer because Jesus told him it was wrong.

—Kate

AFTERMATH

I didn't think the letter warranted a response. I heard he is now married. Hopefully Jesus approves.

CHEAP

WE HAD BEEN DATING
FOR A YEAR AND A
HALF AND HE GAVE ME
$20 IN A CARD FOR
CHRISTMAS.

—Lauren

AFTERMATH

PRETTY SURE HE IS SEEING
SOMEONE ELSE. IF I'M ONLY
WORTH $20, I'D HATE TO SEE
WHAT SHE GETS.

BATTLESTAR GALACTICA

He invited me over to watch the new *Battlestar Galactica* miniseries. After it was over, he declared that the decision to run from the Cylons was cowardly, though he acknowledged that to stay and fight meant the end of the human race. A true patriot would have fought anyway, he said. Then he informed me that the show was obviously anti–Iraq war propaganda, and that he was a fervent supporter of President George W. Bush.

—Shannon

AFTERMATH

I would have ended it right then, but felt bad because we had already purchased tickets to see the premiere of the last *Lord of the Rings* movie with mutual friends a few days later.

PREMARITAL SEX

She kept telling me that I needed to go to church with her. When I asked why, she said, "Because God loves us and only wants us to love and obey him." I asked her how she reconciled our premarital sex with her ortho- dox religiosity and she told me to shut the "F" up.

—Patricio

AFTERMATH

We broke up about a month later. The sex wasn't that good anyway.

THE PROPOSAL

He informed me that he fully intended on proposing to his ex-girlfriend.

—Peg

AFTERMATH

Whatever we had lasted approximately ten minutes after he informed me of this—over breakfast.

FLEA-INFESTED CAT

She took all the money inside our joint account and left me with her flea-infested cat. I hate cats.

—Bernard

AFTERMATH

I had the cat neutered.

RETEACH

SHE TOLD ME
I LOADED THE
DISHWASHER WRONG
AND SHE WAS GOING
TO HAVE TO RETEACH
ME EVERYTHING MY
MOTHER HAD EVER
TAUGHT ME.

—Gone

AFTERMATH

PACKED UP A U-HAUL AND
BOUNCED BACK TO THE
EAST COAST.

DIRT NAP

I came home one night to find him totally smashed and angry about something. In his drunken stupor he told me, "You better be careful, or you're gonna be taking a dirt nap."

—Alive & Well

AFTERMATH

I started looking for a place the next day.

DRUGSTORE COWBOY

HE GAVE ME PINK, GRANDMA-STYLE DRUGSTORE SLIPPERS FOR CHRISTMAS, WITH TASSELS ON THEM, NO LESS. AND THEY WERE THE WRONG SIZE.

—Katy

AFTERMATH

WE BROKE UP THE DAY AFTER CHRISTMAS.

GUILTY CONSCIENCE

He told me that we couldn't move in together because he'd feel guilty when he brought other girls home.

—Natalie

AFTERMATH

Moved in with the guy I was sleeping with before him.

LOSE ME...PLEASE

He called to let me know he wasn't ready to lose me...
or the woman two decades older than me who he had
begun seeing.

—Stormy

AFTERMATH

It lasted as long as it took me to hang up the phone.

LOSE THE JERK INSTEAD

After pursuing me for a while, I finally agreed to date him. After a few dates and sex, he suggested I lose weight and then we could decide where the relationship was going.

—Michele

AFTERMATH

I ran into him a few times but we never dated or had sex again.

LAST RITES

I was out of town because my grandmother was dying. As the priest was giving her the Last Rites, he told me over the phone that it was unfair to him that I had been spending so much time with my family and no time with him over the previous four days. He also wanted to know when the funeral was scheduled to be, so he'd know when I'd be coming back home. She was still alive.

—Mel

AFTERMATH

I hung up on him after calling him selfish, and broke up with him very shortly thereafter.

GUINEA PIG CSI

I found my dead guinea pig behind the couch. He said he "accidentally" killed it while playing with it. I forgave him. A month later he "accidentally" killed another one and disposed of it in the trash can next to the can of ravioli he made right after the "accident."

—Secret

AFTERMATH

I dumped him.

BUT *FRIENDS* IS ON...

When I got pregnant, we couldn't have sex—too risky—so eleven months later I was more than ready. Imagine my surprise when I lit the candles, put on the lingerie, and presented myself to my husband, only to be told, "Um, can we do this tomorrow? It's the season premiere of *Friends* and I don't wanna miss it."

—Vixxen

AFTERMATH

The relationship ended that evening, in my heart anyway, and I asked for a divorce three months later.

PIERCING

I called my boyfriend and heard a noisy background, so I asked where he was. He replied that he was at a piercing place with some friends. As the conversation carried on, I found out he went with a few girls—who I didn't know—to get his penis pierced.

—TLC

AFTERMATH

I told him since he needed a few random girls to hold his penis while it got pierced, he didn't need me. It was over two hours later.

BEAR TRAP

After a summer full of bear sightings, we were walking through my boyfriend's rural backyard when we heard a loud crashing headed in our direction. I turned to him to see if he thought we should run. He'd already grabbed the cat, run back in the house, and was looking out the patio door.

—Amarylis

AFTERMATH

It took me three more years to realize that I should have run…away from him.

GAME ON

I KEPT BEATING HIM IN EVERY VIDEO GAME WE PLAYED AND IT REALLY PISSED HIM OFF. IN THE END, HE TRIED FORBIDDING ME TO PLAY AT ALL.

—Cecilie

AFTERMATH

HE WANTED A GAMER GIRL AND HE GOT ONE. TOO BAD HE WASN'T MAN ENOUGH TO HANDLE IT.

WASH THAT MAN RIGHT OUT OF YOUR HAIR

For my boyfriend's birthday I had gone to a lot of trouble and told him we needed to leave the house by 6:30 or the night's events would be derailed. At 6:30, I was sitting on the couch, ready to go. He came out and whined that his hair wasn't working and said he needed to rewash it. He rewashed it two more times (for a total of *four* hair washings and another hour delay).

—Elizabeth

AFTERMATH

All I could see was how high-maintenance he was and we broke up a few months later.

PURPLE JAWS

The 2009 Golden Globes did a tribute to Steven Spielberg, and he said, "Spielberg didn't direct *Jaws*." I said "What?!" He said, "He may have produced it, but he didn't direct it." Pause. "He didn't direct *The Color Purple*, either."

—Dirks

AFTERMATH

I moved out.

CRAPPY GIFT

After a four-year relationship, he gave me a toilet seat for my birthday present. He said: "I knew you needed one and I couldn't think of what else to get you." And he didn't even wrap it!

—Wanda

AFTERMATH

Unfortunately, I'm reminded of him every day, actually several times a day.

HOURGLASS

I commented that she had a "nice, full, hourglass figure." She snapped, "Oh really…well, perhaps I should do some plus-size modeling!" I went into damage-control mode and tried to clarify my comments but only exacerbated things when I used the term "healthy."

—Kevin

AFTERMATH

With a look of complete disgust, she slapped my face and departed.

THE BIRDS

Birds were chirping outside my window and she complained. I pulled out a pellet gun, and she flipped out. She said, "For future reference, it's always a bad idea to pull out a gun when you have a girl in your bed."

—RS

AFTERMATH

She left and never saw me again.

WAY TO SELL YOURSELF

We had been dating long distance for a couple months when he called to tell me he had just slapped the crap out of some random woman who disagreed with something he had said. He was quite excited about it too.

—Taylor

AFTERMATH

I stopped answering his calls.

NO HABLO ESPAÑOL

I knew it was over when a year and a half into one of my relationships, he told me he failed Spanish class (in college). He was telling me at a moment when he just wanted to share his feelings, he was sad, and I realized that it so turned me off, this utter lack of effort or motivation.

—Carol

AFTERMATH

Of course, I look back and realize how awful I am to men, so unforgiving, without empathy, and I wonder why men date me at all.

I MARRIED A WITCH, LITERALLY

After six years of marriage, two of which saw me as an associate pastor, she announced that she is and had been a practicing Wiccan, complete with a witch name and a regularly scheduled meeting place for her coven.

—Cluelessinohio

AFTERMATH

Three years after our divorce, my girlfriend cut her finger and joked, "Maybe there's a curse on me?"

DEPLOYED

MY SISTER WAS DEPLOYED TO IRAQ. I CRIED. MY BOYFRIEND TOLD ME TO "MAN UP" AND ASKED WHAT I WAS GOING TO MAKE FOR DINNER.

—Marie

AFTERMATH

I TOLD HIM TO PACK HIS STUFF AND GO.

MANNERS

CLAMATO

She was rubbing my shoulders. My shirt was off, allow-
ing me to feel the warm exhale of her belch before I
nosed the cloud of cheeseburger and Clamato gas that
engulfed me. She said nothing and kept humming as if
nothing had happened.

—William

AFTERMATH

It was long distance already, making it easy enough to
just quit.

IT WAS OVER WHEN HE COMPARED MY BREASTS TO A VIDEO GAME.

—RIP

AFTERMATH

IT ENDED THE NEXT MORNING AFTER A YEAR-PLUS OF BEING TOGETHER.

VALENTINE HAZING

It was over when he canceled our dinner plans so he could haze his fraternity's pledges. On Valentine's Day.

—M.

AFTERMATH

I'm never dating a frat boy again.

He made me change my Facebook profile pic because the one I had up wasn't hot enough and he wanted his friends to see how hot I was.

— NotaDoormat

AFTERMATH

Decided I couldn't take any more crap.

MESSAGE SUBTEXT

I went out to dinner with an old girlfriend. Up front, I asked if she was seeing anyone. She replied, "No." After dinner, we went back to my place to watch a movie. She had been rudely texting most of the evening through dinner and our conversations…so I was curious at this "text-pal." I maneuvered to give her a shoulder massage and looked onto her phone and discovered explicit texts to some guy.

—Sally

AFTERMATH

Movie concluded. I drove her home and she asked why I didn't invite her to stay the night…

SPEECHLESS

I was in the middle of a sentence and he started moving his hand in a "talking" motion (fingers and thumb touching together as a mouth opening and closing). He looked straight at me, turned to his hand, and used his other hand to shut it. Apparently, I was supposed to stop talking. I didn't say another word…

—Kelli

AFTERMATH

…until I ended it.

KNEE-HIGH

In real life, my Internet date didn't like to smile, expected me to pay for the entire date, barely spoke, wore knee-high socks with shorts, and had horrible breath. I jumped a curb trying to get away from him.

—rockandroll2442

AFTERMATH

We never spoke again, but he did find me on another social networking site a year and a half later. He pretended not to know who I was, and told me I was attractive and wanted to know if I would like to get together sometime.

THE HORROR, THE HORROR

We were wrapped up in her comforter on the couch post-coitus, watching TV and eating one of those giant chocolate bars. As her hands got smeared with melting chocolate, I watched in horror as she wiped her fingers on the edge of the blanket we were in, then calmly folded over the chocolate-covered corner. I knew it wasn't going to work right there.

—Rob

AFTERMATH

THE RELATIONSHIP LASTED FOR SIX MONTHS, OFF AND ON.

RUG BURN

We were visiting my very conservative parents for the first time. My mother made a comment about getting new carpeting. My girlfriend bent down and rubbed her hand across the floor and exclaimed that this was great "girl carpet" because it's "so soft on your knees!"

—Will

AFTERMATH

This was just one of many times she made these type of comments to see what kind of reaction she'd get. My reaction was to rethink where our relationship was going.

WHITE BALL OF FLAME

HE THREW HIS LEGS OVER HIS SHOULDERS AND PROUDLY LIT A THUNDEROUS FART ON FIRE WITH A LIGHTER.

—Tiff

AFTERMATH

ENDED SHORTLY THEREAFTER, FOR OBVIOUS REASONS. THE WHITE BALL OF FLAME WAS IMPRESSIVE, THOUGH.

CLIPPERS

I noticed he was picking at his toes. A few minutes later, I noticed that he was holding something between his thumb and index finger. Before I knew it, he had put the mystery piece in his mouth and about a minute later I heard a crunch sound. "Are you eating your toenail?" I asked. He looked embarrassed when he said, "Yes, it's a nervous habit of mine."

—Bethany

AFTERMATH

We are actually still living together, but not for much longer.

SANDWICHES

My boyfriend would regularly and gleefully make peanut butter and jelly sandwiches for random homeless drug addicts but wouldn't make me breakfast—or lunch or dinner for that matter—without a huge fight.

—Amy

AFTERMATH

Oddly, he would get angry with me if I made myself food and didn't share it with him. We lasted a tortuous two years.

TARDY

On our second date, I showed up at the designated meeting spot at 7:45 p.m. Forty-five minutes later, he texted me to say he was leaving his apartment and he'd be there soonish, which would have made him an hour and a half late for the date.

—Caramel Party

AFTERMATH

When I told him not to come because I was canceling the date due to his extreme tardiness and disrespect, he says, "What am I supposed to do now?" Hmm, perhaps learn how to not be a douchebag?

HIS FRIENDS

About five months into the relationship, I asked him why I hadn't met any of his friends. He said, "Well, I think you're hot but I think they would say, 'She's not that attractive.'"

—Angela

AFTERMATH

It took me another month or so before I realized I couldn't forgive him and broke up with him via instant message.

ONE, PLEASE

He picked me up, drove us to a movie theater, stepped up to the ticket window, and said, "One, please."

—Shannon

AFTERMATH

No second date.

CHICKEN AND LOTION

He called me up and told me to bring him chicken dinner and also to bring over some lotion so that I could give him a foot rub and a hand-job! I only knew him for a week.

—Jenny

AFTERMATH

I got off the phone with him and changed my number. I only saw him once after that. He tried to flag me down and I floored it.

PERFECT

ONE DAY HE LOOKS
OVER AND SAYS,
"YOU KNOW, YOU'D
BE PERFECT...
WITH GREEN EYES."

—Lucy

AFTERMATH

WE STAYED TOGETHER A YEAR
AND A HALF TO TWO YEARS. THE
COMMENT WAS MADE PRETTY EARLY
ON, BUT IT STUCK WITH ME
THROUGH THE END.

TOO LATE

I was in the hospital miscarrying our child and he told me he'd "be there later" after he got done doing whatever.

—Ladibuggc

AFTERMATH

Things lasted only long enough for me to grieve and then he was done!

A STRETCH

A month into the relationship, we went to the pool and afterward he asked me why I had stretch marks. I said I was probably forty pounds heavier before he knew me. He proceeded with the question, "Did you have a baby?"

—Kat

AFTERMATH

I was seventeen. I was not pregnant, I was just fat. I dumped him a few days later.

HE SAID HE'D CALL ME IN FIVE MINUTES. FIVE MINUTES, FIVE HOURS, FIVE DAYS, FIVE WEEKS, FIVE MONTHS, FIVE YEARS WENT BY AND I NEVER HEARD FROM HIM AGAIN.

—Maria

AFTERMATH

I GUESS THAT WAS THAT.

JEALOUS OF A DEAD GUY

Two days after my best guy friend passed away, my boyfriend said, "Now I probably won't feel jealous anymore."

—Jessica

AFTERMATH

"Probably"? He's *dead.* A week after he got mad at me for continuing to mourn the loss of my friend and said that I should be over it by now. I stopped talking to him that night.

AWKWARD

We had been out on a few dates and I wanted him to meet my best friend and her boyfriend. Everything was going fine until he opened his phone and started showing my best friend all the porn he had downloaded.

—Jillian

AFTERMATH

It was over two weeks later.

YOU GONNA EAT THAT?

My blind date ordered ribs and I ordered chicken. After eating the ribs, with BBQ sauce still all over his face, he started trying to break the bones to suck out the marrow. Then he reached over and started eating from my plate before saying, "You're done with this, right?" He finished our dinner.

—Kat

AFTERMATH

I left him while going to the bathroom.

SNAP

He snapped his fingers at the extremely swamped bartender.

—Jer

AFTERMATH

This was merely a portent of the boorish and exceedingly rude behavior to come that night. After exchanging a horrified look with the bartender and mouthing, "Sorry!" I hurried the date to its conclusion as quickly as possible.

SIZZLER

On our first date, I let her decide where she wanted to eat dinner. She picked Sizzler because she wanted some "good steak." While there she asked the waiter for a job application and proceeded to fill it out at the table during our date.

—Jeremy

AFTERMATH

We still spent the night together, because...well, I'm a guy. But I never talked to her again after that. The whole thing was odd.

DEAR SUBSCRIBER

I was out of town for a close family member's funeral and he wrote me: "Dear subscriber, I know you've been out of town, but your sex balance is past due. Your account will reach virginity status…Please f*ck to avoid disconnection. Thank you. ^-^"

—Kyya

AFTERMATH

That was his sympathy…That was definitely it. We had built our relationship on sex, not much else.

DON'T S*** WHERE YOU EAT... I MEAN...

I had only been married a couple of months and decided to prepare a nice meal for my husband. He was hungry but needed to use the bathroom. So he took his plate into the bathroom and ate it while he was pooping.

—Michelle

AFTERMATH

Divorce!

PARKING NAZI

On our first date as he drove around looking for a parking spot, an elderly couple was slow getting out of their spot, and he started screaming and swearing at them about how slow old people are. He finally gave up on them and proudly pulled into a handicapped parking space as he showed me that he had his "Granny's" parking tag that he can use.

—MLJ

AFTERMATH

I was so embarrassed to be seen with this guy that I ended it quickly after that.

TAINT MY FAULT

HE SCRATCHED HIS
TAINT AND SMELLED
HIS FINGERS.

—Casey

AFTERMATH

HAND SANITIZER.

SORRY, BUDDY

I think it's gonna be over since I found ItWasOverWhen.com written on a piece of paper.

—Kenny

AFTERMATH

Still waiting.

ABOUT THE AUTHOR

Robert K. Elder is a Web entrepreneur and the founder of ItWasOverWhen.com: Tales of Romantic Dead Ends and its sister site ItWasLoveWhen.com: Tales from the Beginning of Love. In June of 2009, Elder started the Web 2.0 company Odd Hours Media, LLC, which launched the user-generated sites. Both went viral very quickly, attracting more than one million hits within a few months.

Elder is also a journalist, author, film columnist, and regional editor of AOL's Patch.com in Chicago. His other books include *The Film That Changed My Life: 30 Directors on Their Epiphanies in the Dark* and *Last Words of the Executed*.

His work has appeared in the *New York Times*, MSNBC.com, the *Los Angeles Times*, Salon.com, and many other publications. For almost a decade, he served as a staff writer at the *Chicago Tribune*. Elder also teaches multimedia journalism at Northwestern University's Medill School.

A Montana native and graduate of the University of Oregon, Elder lives and writes in Chicagoland with his lovely bride and their twins.

He has been known to carry a digital voice recorder.

You can follow ItWasOverWhen.com via Twitter for daily updates @overwhen, and you can follow its sister website @lovewhen. Elder's own Twitter address is @robertkelder, and you can also reach him via his website at www.robertkelder.com.

IT WAS LOVE WHEN...

Tales from the Beginning of Love

Robert K. Elder

PENGUIN

He told me I was a penguin, "tiny, adorable, and loved by everyone."

—Taylor

POSTSCRIPT

He moved across the country, went to college, and found another girl. But I still love him.

STARS

After we spent the night together, we couldn't spend the day together because he "had things to do." Later that night, we were lying together in his bed, snuggling and reading together, when suddenly he turned off the lights and told me to look up at the ceiling. Glow-in-the-dark stars covered the entire ceiling, spelling out "I love you."

—Iris

POSTSCRIPT

He'd spent the whole day working on it! I told him that I loved him too, and we've been together ever since.

978-1-4022-5671-4 • $12.99 U.S.
Coming Fall 2011